UNBELIEVABLE

FOOTBALL

WORLD FOOTBALL WINNERS!

For Arlo and Lila.

The stories in this collection were first published in a different form in
Unbelievable Football 2: How Football Can Change the World in 2021 and
*Unbelievable Football: The Most Incredible True Football Stories –
The England Edition* in 2022 by Wren & Rook.

This collection first published in 2026.

ISBN: 978 1 5263 6761 7

1 3 5 7 9 10 8 6 4 2

MIX
Paper | Supporting
responsible forestry
FSC
www.fsc.org
FSC® C104740

Wren & Rook
An imprint of
Hachette Children's Group
Part of Hodder & Stoughton Limited
Carmelite House
50 Victoria Embankment
London EC4Y 0DZ

The authorised representative in the EEA is Hachette Ireland, 8 Castlecourt Centre,
Dublin 15, D15 XTP3, Ireland (email: info@hbgi.ie).

An Hachette UK Company
www.hachette.co.uk
www.hachettechildrens.co.uk

Printed in China.

MATT OLDFIELD

ILLUSTRATED BY
DANIEL DUNCAN

3 AMAZING TRUE STORIES

UNBELIEVABLE
FOOTBALL

WORLD FOOTBALL WINNERS!

wren & rook

CONTENTS

INTRODUCTION   7
Welcome to *World Football Winners!*

FIRST HALF   11
Food, friends and football

HALF TIME   39
Five fast facts about the World Cup

SECOND HALF 47

The amazing tournament
for children!

EXTRA TIME 61

Football's greatest villain,
or hero?

INTRODUCTION

Welcome to
World Football Winners!

Get ready to read three of the most amazing tales in world football.

The first half is about the first-ever Women's World Cup, which was full of football, food and **friendship**.

The second half is about the **amazing** Street Child World Cup. Read all about ordinary young people from around the world, playing against each other in an amazing football tournament.

At half time, there are **incredible** facts to discover about World Cup football through the years.

Finally, in extra time, there's one last twist in the tale, with a story about Argentinian player Diego Maradona's sneaky 'Hand of God' moment in the World Cup quarter-finals.

So, what are you waiting for?

It's time for kick-off!

FIRST HALF

Food, friends and football

The **first-ever Women's World Cup** took place in 1991. It was full of great goals, super saves and **amazing action**. It happened sixty-one years after the first men's competition, because for a long time, women weren't encouraged to play football at all. Women's football was **banned** in a lot of countries, and only men were allowed to play in teams or tournaments.

How unfair!

Luckily, the Women's World Cup in 1991 was part of a **big change** in thinking. It took place in China, and twelve teams were involved, from all over the world:

- China, Japan and Chinese Taipei, from Asia
- New Zealand, from Oceania
- Nigeria, from Africa
- Denmark, Germany, Italy, Norway and Sweden, from Europe
- Brazil, from South America
- USA, from North America

It was a very **important moment** for women's football. The pressure was on to prove to the people in charge of the game that this World Cup should be more than just a one-time event.

Norway and Sweden were the favourites to win it, but Team USA had lots of talented players.

They also had two other things in their favour: fitness and food.

Food?

Yes, food!

The USA team had played at a smaller women's football tournament, before, which was also held in China. Back then, with only a small food budget, the team had found eating tricky.

They **couldn't afford** to eat at yummy restaurants, and the hotel food wasn't great. They ended up living on fizzy drinks and chocolate instead. That might sound delicious, but it's not the best if you want to be on **top form** playing football!

Three years later, they decided to take their own cooks with them. The team hadn't suddenly become highly paid superstars; the cooks that came with them were family members who had agreed to do it for free!

'Fill the suitcases with pasta! Let's feed them all the way to victory,' the cooks cheered!

While the USA players were well prepared for the World Cup, **their opponents weren't**. The Swedish team were staying in the same hotel, with the yucky hotel food. When they found out about the **secret** pasta stash, they **cheekily** asked:

'Can we have some too?'

That's a tough one – what would you say if one of your football club's **biggest** rivals asked to share your food supplies? Yes or no? The USA were even playing against Sweden in their very first group game, which must have made the decision **even tougher**.

But remember, all of the teams at the tournament were working **together** towards the same goal of standing up for women's football.

'We'll share our pasta with you!' the USA team told Sweden.

How kind of them!

And guess what? Good things happen to
good people. The USA beat Sweden 3–2,
and that was them just getting started.

After that, they **succeeded** against every opponent! In the group stage they beat Brazil 5–0 and Japan 3–0.

In the quarter-finals, Team USA player Michelle Akers **dashed**, **darted** and **swooped** her way to an impressive five goals against Chinese Taipei. The **amazing** match finished in a 7–0 victory.

Germany put up a **good fight** in the semi-finals, but they were still **no match** for the USA. Carin Jennings fired in **three great goals**, and April Heinrichs added two more in a 5–2 win.

Full of pasta but still **hungry for glory** – it turned out to be a real recipe for success!

With twenty-two goals scored in only five games, the USA were entertaining everyone – even the people who weren't supportive of the tournament! **They'd made it through to the first-ever Women's World Cup final!**

There, in front of 63,000 fans, the USA faced Norway. With **fifteen minutes to go**, the score was still 1–1. There could only be one **World Cup winner**, but which team would it be?

In what were an **incredible** few moments of **action**, Team USA striker Michelle Akers chased after the ball using the last of her pasta energy …

Akers **slipped past** Norway's defenders with **incredible speed**.

The Norweigan goalkeeper dived for the ball,
but Akers dribbled around her …

Soon it was all over …

Akers tapped the ball into the empty net…

GOALLLL!!

2–1 to Team USA. They were the new **World Champions!**

'Go, Team USA!'

After celebrating on the pitch, the players returned to their hotel to rest. As the lift door opened, they found a very special banner waiting for them on the floor ...
guess what it said?

The word **'CONGRATULATIONS'** spelled out in socks!

'Wow! Who has left us such a kind message?' the players wondered.

There was a big clue in the colour of the socks.

They were yellow, **Sweden's colour!**
Despite losing to USA , they wanted to say well
done to the winners **(plus thank you for
the dinners!)**.

It might have been a bit stinky –

PE-EWWW, socks!

However, have you ever heard a better example
of **sporting behaviour** than that?

Entertaining football?

Tick!

Food and friendship?

Tick!

The first-ever Women's World Cup had been a **huge success**, and from there, the competition **grew** and **grew**. Sixteen teams took part in the 1999 World Cup, and thirty-two teams took part in the 2023 competition.

The audience grew too: **over 220 million** people around the world watched Spain beat England in the 2023 Women's World Cup final.

What a great **success** story for women's football. The players really **achieved their goal**, proving that the Women's World Cup was here to stay!

HURRAY!

Five fast facts about the World Cup

Time to take a half-time break!

What's better than five quick facts about World Cup football to get you ready for the second half?

1 Did you know that the **very first** men's World Cup was organised by **FIFA** in 1930? It was hosted by Uruguay, in South America. Playing at home must have been **lucky** for them, because they won, beating Argentina 4–2 in the final.

2 Since the beginning of the men's World Cup in 1930, there have been **only two trophies**. The first was called the Jules Rimet World Cup trophy and it was **awarded until 1970**. The second is called the FIFA World Cup trophy and has been **awarded from 1974 to today**.

3 Did you know that the USA is the **most successful** FIFA Women's World Cup team? They have **won** the tournament **four times** since 1991!

4 Some **big names** have played in the World Cup over the years. Two of the **biggest** goalscorers ever are German player Miroslav Klose, who **scored** sixteen goals across twenty-four games, and Brazilian player Marta who scored an **impressive** seventeen goals across twenty-three matches.

5 Did you know that FIFA also organise the FIFA Beach Soccer World Cup? Beach soccer is a form of five-a-side football played on a **beach** or sand. The first-ever FIFA Beach Soccer World Cup took place in Rio de Janeiro in 2005, and a tournament has taken place every two years since 2009! I wonder if the winners get to have a nice ice cream for afters?

Yum!

SECOND HALF

The amazing tournament for children

The Street Child World Cup takes place every four years, just like the FIFA World Cup. But instead of professional footballers, **it's played by children!**

It was set up in 2010 by charity workers in South Africa. They wanted to do something to **help children** living on the streets there. There are lots of children **all over the world** who don't have homes. Some of them never have the chance to see a doctor, or the option of going to school.

To make the event as fun as possible, they decided it would involve football:

Everyone's favourite sport!

They made some simple rules for the tournament. Each team had to have a mix of boys and girls aged fourteen to sixteen who had lived on the streets. After spreading the news far and wide, **eight countries signed up** to compete in the very first tournament in South Africa, in 2010:

- Tanzania and the hosts, South Africa, came from Africa
- India, Philippines and Vietnam came from Asia
- Nicaragua came from Central America
- Ukraine and England came from Europe

'*This tournament will show that we can do amazing things.*'

– Dennis David, one of the players from Tanzania

The **exciting** seven-a-side matches were held in the evenings. During the days, the kids were **free to have fun!** They went to the beach, went to a safari park and spent time at local schools. They **learnt about each other** and shared stories and ideas through art and football.

Sounds like the **best trip ever**, doesn't it? Thinking ahead to the future, each country's team came up with lists of **changes** they needed that would **improve their lives**. They also teamed up with the other countries, **demanding** that their voices be heard and for street children all around the world to be **protected**.

But – we can't forget about the football, can we? Do you want to know **who won** the football tournament? Well, the first-ever Street Child World Cup final took place between India and Tanzania.

As the game neared its end, the score was still 0–0. But at the **last minute**, India received a penalty. The Tanzanian keeper couldn't quite reach the ball …

AND IT WAS A GOAL!

The score was 1–0 and India were the winners of the 2010 Street Child World Cup. **Well done, India**. But really, in the end, all of the children were **winners**, too!

The tournament was a **huge success**. The children returned to their countries feeling less lonely and worried, and more **determined** to fight for their rights.

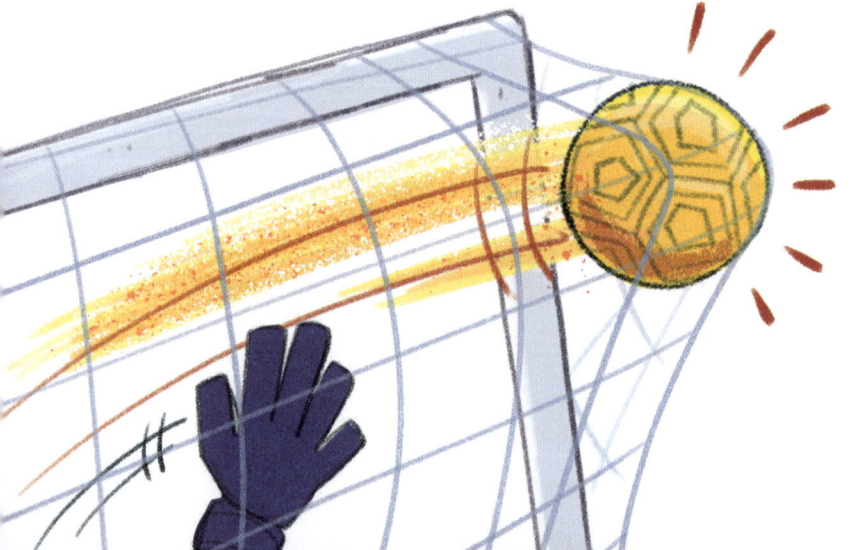

Four years later, the second Street Child World Cup took place in Brazil. This time it was even **bigger!** There were 230 children involved from 19 different countries.

It featured separate tournaments for boys and girls. Tanzania won the boys' final, and the hosts, Brazil, lifted the girls' trophy.

Once again, football was **helping** to bring young people **together** to fight for a better future. The Street Child World Cup raised an important issue and spread a **very powerful** message:

Everyone deserves to be treated equally.

At the 2018 tournament, away from the pitch, one player from each of the twenty-three teams stood up and **gave a speech** about the problems for street children in their country, and what football can do to help. They were all **fantastic**, but this one by Hendra from the Philippines is my favourite:

'We are the avengers. Why avengers? Because we have faced many challenges and obstacles in our lives. But still we continue to walk the path towards our future.'

Do you have a favourite superhero or supervillain?

Well, sometimes even football players get reputations as **heroes or villains!** A player can go from hero to villain and back again, sometimes all within the same match. There's one villain who **shines** above the rest for the England football team and fans, though: **Argentina's Diego Armando Maradona.**

At the 1986 World Cup in Mexico, Maradona – the **'Golden Boy'** from Buenos Aires – was a **football wizard** at the peak of his power. He was simply **unstoppable**. He led Argentina all the way through to the quarter-finals, where they would face England.

During the first half in Mexico City, England managed to keep Maradona pretty quiet thanks to a few fair tackles and a lot of fouls.

We've got this! the England team thought.

Early in the second half, however, Maradona burst into life, changing the course of the game in just four minutes.

First, Maradona **dropped deep** to get the ball, and then with a **clever** change of speed, he **burst** between two England midfielders before **gliding** past another. With two big defenders blocking his path, Maradona tried to pass the ball to an Argentina striker. England player Steve Hodge **intercepted it**, but he could only flick the ball up into the air and towards his **own goal** …

Maradona kept running forwards. As the ball dropped down in the penalty area, the England keeper came out to punch it away, but Maradona **leapt up and knocked it past him**.

'**GOAL!**' Argentina cheered.

So why were all the England players waving their arms in the air and running towards the referee?

They were complaining because Maradona hadn't scored with his head. Maradona had **scored with his left hand**, which was hidden behind his head!

'Handball!' all the England players exclaimed.

'Surely the goal will be disallowed and a free kick given?' they asked.

But **no**, somehow the referee hadn't spotted Maradona's handball. **Maradona celebrated!** He even had the **cheek** to run around with his left hand raised in the air, until his teammates told him to stop.

The England team and all their fans couldn't believe it – Maradona had **cheated** and got away with it!

If only there had been a video referee back then. The players complained and the fans booed – **they had a new number one supervillain!**

But just four minutes after his handball, Maradona scored what would soon be called the **'Goal of the Century'**.

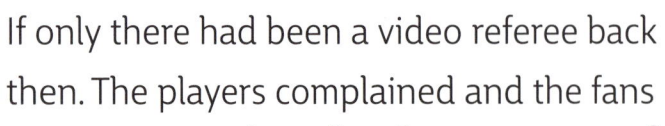

With three quick touches, Maradona spun away from his opponents, and **ZOOM!** he was off, over the halfway line and towards goal.

'Uh-oh, we're in serious trouble now.' The England players were worried!

Maradona then tricked his way past the two England defenders. **What a run!** There was still one defender left to beat, but Maradona fooled him too, just like he'd fooled the rest of his teammates.

As he faked to shoot, the England keeper dived down, and Maradona just dribbled around him and guided the ball into the empty net.

'GOAL!'

I'll let Maradona finish the story himself: **'I'd scored the goal of my life.'**

England managed to score a late goal, but it wasn't enough. Thanks to those two moments of **trickery from Maradona** – one with his left hand, the other with his left foot – Argentina were through to the semi-finals, and they went on to **win the World Cup**.

After the final whistle, the England players shook hands with their Argentinian opponents, but most were too upset to swap shirts.

When the England manager walked into the dressing room after the match, there was one thing still on his mind.

'He did handball it, didn't he?' he called out to his players.

'Yes!' everyone cried.

So, did Maradona ever feel bad about what he'd done? Oh no, not even a little bit. He was willing to do anything to win. After the match, he joked that the goal was scored:

'A little with the head of Maradona, and a little with the hand of God'.

For some people, Maradona will always be a villain. For others, he is one of the greatest football heroes ever! What do you think? Either way, he was a very skilled and entertaining player!

FULL TIME

Sources

Football, Food and Friendship at the 1991 FIFA Women's World Cup

Theivam, Kieran & Kassouf, Jeff. *The Making of the Women's World Cup* (London: Robinson, 2019).

Welcome to the Street Child World Cup!

David, Dennis. Quote reproduced in 'Street children find hope in football.' FIFA.com. 19 March 2010. www.fifa.com/worldcup/news/street-children-find-hope-football-1183006, accessed 11 May 2021.
Hendra. Quote reproduced in 'Street Child World Cup Moscow 2018.' Street Child United. www.streetchildunited.org/our-sports-events/past-events/street-child-world-cup-moscow-2018/,accessed 11 May 2021.

1986: Maradona's Hand of God

Maradona, Diego. *El Diego* (London: Yellow Jersey, 2005).

Winter, Henry. *Fifty Years of Hurt* (London: Bantam Press, 2016).

Barry Davies and Terry Butcher quotes from *The Hand of God: 30 Years On*. ITV Documentaries, 22 June 2016.

'Diego Maradona: Argentina legend's "Hand of God" shirt wells for £7.1 million at auction.' BBC Sport, 4 May 2022. https://www.bbc.co.uk/sport/football/61321555, accessed 10 May 2022.

UNBELIEVABLE FOOTBALL

COLOUR SHORT STORIES

If you enjoyed these stories, look out for more true football tales in this series:

Superstar Strikers!

Animal Antics!

World Football Winners!

Trophy Triumphs!

Inspiring Heroes!

For more incredible football
fun, why not try these books
by Matt Oldfield:

Unbelievable Football
**The Most Incredible True
Football Stories
(You Never Knew)**

Unbelievable Football 2
**How Football Can Change
The World**

Unbelievable Football
The England Edition

The Unbelievable Football Trivia Book
Facts, Stats, Jokes, Quizzes and More!

Unbelievable Football
Five-Minute Amazing True Stories

Unbelievable Football
365 Amazing True Stories

Football Spy
Red Card

Unbelievable Football
World of Football